100 INSPIRATIONAL QUOTES - FOUND LOST SEARCH

GALERON PRESS

GALERON CONSULTING

Contents

Introduction

Welcome to this collection of 100 inspirational quotes, carefully se-
lected from the pages of "Lost Found Search: The Self-Improvement
Handbook - Mastering the Art of Personal Growth." This book has
been a labor of love and a testament to the transformative power of
self-improvement. These quotes are meant to serve as a beacon of
hope, wisdom, and encouragement as you embark on your journey
towards personal growth and self-discovery.

Each quote has been handpicked from the various chapters and
sections of the book, focusing on the key themes of self-awareness,
goal-setting, time management, resilience, adaptability, and maintain-
ing inspiration and motivation for long-term success. These quotes
encapsulate the essence of the book's teachings, providing a snapshot
of the profound insights and life-changing lessons contained within
its pages.

These 100 quotes are more than just words on a page; they are a re-
flection of the trials, tribulations, and triumphs that we all experience
on our journey towards self-improvement. They serve as a reminder
that we are not alone in our quest for personal growth, and that with
dedication, perseverance, and the right mindset, we can overcome any
obstacle and achieve our goals.

We encourage you to read through these quotes at your own pace,
allowing the words to resonate with you and inspire you to take action

in your own life. You may even choose to revisit them from time to time, using them as a source of motivation and encouragement when you need a little extra push to keep moving forward.

As you read through these quotes, remember that the journey of self-improvement is a personal one, unique to each individual. Embrace your journey, learn from your experiences, and let these words of wisdom guide you towards a brighter, more fulfilling future.

Here's to your growth, success, and the boundless potential that lies within each and every one of us.

Chapter 1

"The journey of personal growth begins with self-awareness."

Becoming aware of your thoughts, emotions, and behaviors is the first step towards making positive changes in your life.

Chapter 2

"Embrace change as an opportunity for growth and self-discovery."

Change is inevitable; by seeing it as an opportunity, you open yourself up to new experiences and personal development.

Chapter 3

"You are the architect of your own life — design it with intention."

Your life is in your hands; take control and make conscious choices to create a fulfilling and purposeful existence.

Chapter 4

"Cherish the small victories, as they lead to significant transformations."

Every little success counts, and each one brings you closer to your ultimate goals.

Chapter 5

"The power to overcome obstacles lies within you."

You have the strength and resilience to face any challenge and come out stronger on the other side.

Chapter 6

"Developing a growth mindset will unlock your full potential."

By embracing the idea that you can improve and learn, you open yourself up to endless possibilities for personal growth.

Chapter 7

"Setbacks are temporary — use them as stepping stones to success."

Learn from your setbacks and use the lessons to propel you forward on your journey to success.

Chapter 8

"Invest in yourself, for you are your most valuable asset."

Prioritize self-care, personal growth, and self-improvement to create a fulfilling and successful life.

Chapter 9

"Your self-worth is not determined by external factors — you are enough."

Remember that your value comes from within and is not dependent on external validation.

Chapter 10

"Unlock your full potential by challenging limiting beliefs."

Identify and overcome self-limiting beliefs to tap into your hidden strengths and capabilities.

Chapter 11

"Success is a journey, not a destination — savor every moment."

Embrace the process and enjoy the experiences along the way to achieving your goals.

Chapter 12

"Surround yourself with people who uplift and inspire you."

Build a support network of positive, like-minded individuals who encourage your growth and success.

Chapter 13

"Cultivate gratitude to transform your mindset and your life."

Practicing gratitude can shift your focus from what you lack to the abundance in your life, fostering happiness and contentment.

Chapter 14

"The key to effective communication lies in empathy and active listening."

Develop your listening skills and practice empathy to foster deeper connections and better understanding in your relationships.

Chapter 15

"Your past does not define you — let go of what no longer serves you."

Release the burdens of the past and focus on the present moment to create a brighter future.

Chapter 16
"Set clear goals and develop a roadmap to success."

Having a clear vision and actionable steps will help you stay focused and motivated on your journey to success.

Chapter 17

"Embrace your authentic self and let your unique light shine."

Be true to yourself, celebrate your individuality, and share your gifts with the world.

Chapter 18

"Seek balance in all aspects of your life to achieve harmony and well-being."

Strive for balance between work, relationships, and personal growth to create a fulfilling and contented life.

Chapter 19

"Nurture your relationships with care, compassion, and understanding."

Healthy, supportive relationships are essential for personal growth and happiness; invest time and effort in cultivating them.

Chapter 20

"Make time for self-reflection to gain insights and foster growth."

Regular self-reflection can help you identify areas for improvement and create a roadmap for personal growth.

Chapter 21

"Choose your battles wisely – not every conflict is worth your energy."

Prioritize your well-being and focus on the issues that truly matter in the long run.

"Celebrate the journey of personal growth, recognizing that each step you take brings you closer to your best self."

Embrace the process of personal growth and the lessons it provides, understanding that every experience contributes to your ongoing development and self-improvement.

Chapter 23

"Your thoughts shape your reality — choose them wisely."

Be mindful of your thought patterns, as they have the power to influence your experiences and overall well-being.

Chapter 24
"Self-discipline is the cornerstone of success."

Cultivating self-discipline will empower you to achieve your goals and maintain a healthy, balanced lifestyle.

Chapter 25

"Trust the process — sometimes the greatest lessons come from unexpected sources."

Keep an open mind and embrace the lessons that life presents, even when they come from unexpected places.

Chapter 26

"Celebrate your uniqueness — you are a one-of-a-kind masterpiece."

Embrace your individuality and honor the unique qualities that make you who you are.

Chapter 27

"Develop a strong sense of purpose to guide your actions and decisions."

Having a clear purpose in life will provide direction and motivation, helping you navigate your personal growth journey.

Chapter 28

"Resilience is the key to overcoming adversity and achieving success."

Strengthen your ability to bounce back from setbacks and use them as fuel for growth and achievement.

Chapter 29

"Forgive yourself and others — let go of grudges and embrace healing."

Forgiveness is a powerful tool for healing and personal growth, allowing you to release negative emotions and move forward with a lighter heart.

Chapter 30

"Transform your fears into opportunities for growth."

Confront your fears head-on and use them as catalysts for personal development and self-discovery.

Chapter 31

"Cultivate a positive attitude — it's a powerful force for change."

A positive mindset can help you overcome challenges, achieve your goals, and improve your overall well-being.

Chapter 32

"Your time is precious — use it wisely and intentionally."

Prioritize activities and commitments that align with your values and contribute to your personal growth.

Chapter 33

"Empower yourself with knowledge and never stop learning."

Seek out new experiences, ideas, and perspectives to expand your horizons and promote personal growth.

Chapter 34

"Be patient with yourself — personal growth is a lifelong journey."

Give yourself the time and space to learn, grow, and evolve at your own pace.

Chapter 35

"Create a supportive environment that fosters growth and success."

Surround yourself with positive influences and resources that encourage your personal development journey.

Chapter 36

"Visualize your success and take action to make it a reality."

Envisioning your goals and taking consistent steps towards them will help you achieve the life you desire.

Chapter 37

"The only person you should compare yourself to is the person you were yesterday."

Focus on your own progress and growth, rather than comparing yourself to others.

Chapter 38

"Find joy in the process of growth, not just the end result."

Enjoy the journey of self-improvement and embrace the lessons and experiences along the way.

Chapter 39

"Cultivate self-compassion — treat yourself with the same kindness and understanding you'd offer a friend."

Practice self-compassion to nurture your emotional well-being and promote personal growth.

Chapter 40

"Take responsibility for your life and your actions."

Owning your choices and their consequences empowers you to make positive changes and create the life you desire.

Chapter 41

"Never underestimate the power of a small, consistent effort."

Persistent effort, even in small increments, can lead to significant growth and achievement over time.

Chapter 42

"Embrace vulnerability as a source of strength and connection."

By allowing yourself to be vulnerable, you open yourself up to deeper connections and personal growth opportunities.

Chapter 43

"Success is not final, failure is not fatal — it's the courage to continue that counts."

Keep pushing forward, regardless of setbacks or achievements, to continue your personal growth journey.

"Believe in your ability to grow, change, and achieve your dreams."

Chapter 44

"Believe in your ability to grow, change, and achieve your dreams."

Cultivate self-confidence and trust in your potential to overcome challenges and accomplish your goals.

Chapter 45

"Seek out mentors and role models who inspire you to grow."

Surround yourself with individuals who motivate you and offer valuable guidance on your personal growth journey.

Chapter 46

"Take time for self-care — you can't pour from an empty cup."

Prioritize self-care to maintain your physical, emotional, and mental well-being, enabling you to better support your personal growth journey.

Chapter 47

"Growth happens outside of your comfort zone – dare to take risks."

Embrace new experiences and step out of your comfort zone to unlock your full potential and foster personal growth.

Chapter 48

"Every moment is an opportunity for growth and self-improvement."

Seize each moment as a chance to learn, grow, and make positive changes in your life.

Chapter 49

"Embrace the power of positive affirmations to reframe your mindset."

Use positive affirmations to shift your thought patterns and cultivate a mindset conducive to personal growth.

Chapter 50
"Find your tribe — connect with like-minded individuals who share your passion for growth."

Seek out communities and friendships that support and encourage your personal growth journey.

Chapter 51

"Success is a habit — develop routines that support your growth and well-being."

Establish habits and rituals that nurture your personal growth and contribute to a balanced, successful life.

Chapter 52

"Learn to embrace and manage stress as a catalyst for growth."

Develop healthy coping mechanisms and strategies to turn stress into a driving force for personal development.

Chapter 53

"Your intuition is a powerful guide — trust it and follow its wisdom."

Tune into your inner wisdom and trust your intuition to guide you on your personal growth journey.

Chapter 54

"Stay curious and open to new ideas, experiences, and perspectives."

Cultivate a curious and open-minded attitude to foster continuous learning and personal growth.

Chapter 55

"Take ownership of your emotions and choose how to respond to them."

Acknowledge your emotions and decide how to react to them, empowering you to take control of your emotional well-being.

Chapter 56

"Create a vision board to inspire and motivate you on your personal growth journey."

Use visualization techniques, like a vision board, to keep your goals and dreams front and center, motivating you to stay on track.

Chapter 57

"Be proactive in seeking opportunities for growth and development."

Actively search for and seize opportunities to learn, evolve, and make progress on your personal growth journey.

Chapter 58

"Embrace failure as a valuable learning experience."

View failure as an essential part of growth and use the lessons learned to improve and progress.

Chapter 59

"Find balance in giving and receiving — nurture yourself as well as others."

Maintain a healthy balance between caring for yourself and supporting others, to ensure your own growth and well-being.

Chapter 60

"Cultivate a sense of wonder and awe to enrich your life."

Embrace the beauty and wonder of life, allowing it to inspire and invigorate your personal growth journey.

Chapter 61

"Practice mindfulness to stay present and fully engaged in your life."

Develop mindfulness skills to stay grounded in the present moment, fostering greater awareness and personal growth.

Chapter 62

"Develop resilience by facing challenges head-on and learning from them."

Build resilience by tackling difficulties with courage and determination, gaining valuable insights and fostering personal growth.

Chapter 63

"Celebrate your victories, no matter how small they may seem."

Acknowledge and appreciate your accomplishments, as they are milestones on your personal growth journey.

Chapter 64

"Set clear boundaries to protect your energy and well-being."

Establish healthy boundaries to safeguard your mental, emotional, and physical health, supporting your personal growth.

Chapter 65

"Practice gratitude to cultivate a positive outlook and attract abundance."

Embrace gratitude as a daily habit, shifting your perspective and attracting more positivity and growth into your life.

Chapter 66

"Learn to let go of what no longer serves you — make space for growth."

Release anything that hinders your personal growth, creating room for new opportunities and experiences.

Chapter 67

"Reflect on your progress and adjust your goals as needed."

Regularly review your personal growth journey, evaluating your progress and adjusting your goals to stay aligned with your aspirations.

Chapter 68

"Continuously learn and expand your knowledge to fuel your growth."

Commit to lifelong learning and self-education, constantly expanding your knowledge and skills to support your personal growth.

Chapter 69

"Recognize the power of your thoughts — choose to think positively."

Be aware of your thought patterns, consciously choosing to focus on positive and empowering thoughts that support your growth.

Chapter 70

"Cultivate self-awareness to better understand and improve yourself."

Develop self-awareness to gain insights into your strengths, weaknesses, and areas for growth, guiding your personal development journey.

Chapter 71

"Embrace vulnerability as a pathway to deeper connections and growth."

Allow yourself to be vulnerable, opening up to authentic relationships and experiences that foster personal growth.

Chapter 72

"Nourish your body, mind, and spirit for optimal well-being and growth."

Prioritize your holistic well-being by nurturing your physical, mental, and spiritual health to support your personal growth journey.

Chapter 73

"Harness the power of visualization to manifest your goals and dreams."

Use visualization techniques to create mental images of your desired outcomes, fueling your motivation and personal growth.

Chapter 74

"Set SMART goals to create a clear roadmap for your personal growth journey."

Develop Specific, Measurable, Achievable, Relevant, and Time-bound goals to guide your personal growth and ensure success.

Chapter 75

"Cultivate self-compassion and embrace your imperfections."

Practice self-compassion by acknowledging your imperfections and treating yourself with kindness and understanding as you grow.

Chapter 76

"Embrace change and see it as an opportunity for growth."

Welcome change in your life, viewing it as a chance for personal growth and development rather than fearing it.

Chapter 77

"Invest in yourself by seeking out resources, experiences, and connections that support your growth."

Prioritize your personal growth by dedicating time, energy, and resources to activities and relationships that contribute to your development.

Chapter 78

"Establish a growth mindset and embrace challenges as opportunities to learn."

Cultivate a growth mindset, believing in your ability to learn, grow, and adapt in the face of challenges and setbacks.

Chapter 79

"Develop a strong sense of purpose to guide and motivate your personal growth journey."

Clarify your purpose in life to provide direction and motivation for your personal growth and development.

Chapter 80

"Balance your need for personal growth with self-acceptance and contentment."

Strive for personal growth while also appreciating your current self and finding contentment in the present moment.

Chapter 81

"Take calculated risks and push beyond your comfort zone to facilitate growth."

Embrace risk-taking and stepping outside your comfort zone as essential components of personal growth and development.

Chapter 82

"Develop a strong support network to share your journey and learn from others."

Create and nurture a network of supportive individuals who can provide guidance, encouragement, and inspiration on your personal growth journey.

Chapter 83

"Prioritize self-care and create healthy habits to support your well-being and growth."

Dedicate time and energy to self-care, developing healthy habits that nurture your well-being and facilitate personal growth.

Chapter 84

"Develop a daily routine that incorporates activities and practices that support your growth."

Establish a daily routine that includes personal growth activities, such as reading, journaling, meditation, and exercise.

Chapter 85

"Believe in your potential and have faith in your ability to grow and evolve."

Trust in your innate capacity for growth, evolution, and transformation, and believe in your ability to achieve your goals.

Chapter 86

"Seek feedback and constructive criticism to learn from others and improve."

Embrace feedback and criticism as opportunities to learn, grow, and refine your skills and knowledge.

Chapter 87

"Create a vision for your life that inspires you and aligns with your values."

Develop a compelling vision for your future that reflects your core values and motivates you to pursue personal growth.

Chapter 88

"Practice mindfulness to cultivate greater self-awareness and presence."

Engage in mindfulness practices to enhance self-awareness, presence, and emotional intelligence, supporting your personal growth journey.

Chapter 89

"Acknowledge and celebrate your achievements, no matter how small they may seem."

Recognize and appreciate your progress and accomplishments, as this reinforces your motivation and commitment to personal growth.

Chapter 90

"Be patient with yourself, recognizing that personal growth is a lifelong journey."

Understand that personal growth is an ongoing process, and grant yourself the patience and time needed to evolve and develop.

Chapter 91

"Learn from your mistakes and use them as opportunities for growth."

Embrace your mistakes as valuable learning experiences that contribute to your personal development and growth.

Chapter 92

"Stay curious and open-minded, always seeking new knowledge and experiences."

Maintain an attitude of curiosity and openness, actively pursuing new information, perspectives, and experiences that support your growth.

Chapter 93

"Cultivate resilience to bounce back from setbacks and challenges."

Develop the ability to recover from adversity and setbacks, using these experiences as catalysts for personal growth and development.

Chapter 94

"Nurture positive relationships that support and encourage your growth."

Invest in relationships with people who uplift and inspire you, fostering a supportive environment that promotes personal growth.

Chapter 95

"Develop strong communication skills to effectively express yourself and connect with others."

Hone your communication skills to enhance your relationships, improve your understanding, and support your personal and professional growth.

Chapter 96

"Practice gratitude to cultivate a positive mindset and appreciate your growth journey."

Embrace gratitude as a powerful tool for fostering positivity, contentment, and appreciation for your personal growth journey.

Chapter 97

"Embrace lifelong learning as a fundamental aspect of personal growth."

Commit to ongoing learning and self-improvement, understanding that personal growth is a lifelong endeavor.

Chapter 98

"Remember that you are the architect of your own life, and your growth is in your hands."

Empower yourself with the knowledge that you have the ability to shape your life and personal growth journey, taking responsibility for your development and progress.

Chapter 99

"Surround yourself with positive energy and environments that uplift you."

Seek out positive people, places, and experiences that inspire and support your personal growth journey.

Chapter 100

"Take responsibility for your life and choices — you have the power to create change."

Embrace your personal power by taking charge of your life and making conscious choices that support your growth.

Chapter 101

"Challenge limiting beliefs and replace them with empowering thoughts."101

Identify and confront self-limiting beliefs, replacing them with positive, growth-oriented thoughts to propel your personal development.

www.ingramcontent.com/pod-product-compliance
Lightning Source LLC
Chambersburg PA
CBHW071236020426

42333CB00015B/1500